TACTICS

KILL OR BE KILLED

In the struggle to survive, many animals have become killer creatures, attacking to defend themselves or to satisfy their hunger. Some are solitary hunters, while others co-operate in packs or even armies. Few corners of the Earth – in the air, in water or on land – are safe from predators.

Sharks

A great white lives up to its nickname, 'Jaws', as it grabs a mouthful of tuna. The great white is the ultimate ocean predator. Like other killer sharks, it relies on its senses, speed and terrifying power to locate and overwhelm seals and other prey.

- Location: almost all oceans
- Habitat: coastal waters
- Length: 6m

Big cats

A bloodied Bengal tiger reveals its fearsome fangs. Tigers, lions and other big cats use stealth, speed and sheer power to bring down prey, such as deer.

- Location: southern Asia
- Habitat: rainforest, forests and grasslands
- Length: 3m

Raptors

A harpy eagle makes off with a howler monkey. Eagles, hawks and falcons are the killers of the bird world. Known as raptors, they use their talons to stab prey and their beaks to rip apart flesh.

- Location: North and South America
- Habitat: lowland rainforest
- Wingspan: 2m

 > A harpy eagle is armed with super-sharp talons that are up to 13cm long – almost as long as a grizzly bear's claws.

Wolves

A grey wolf tears into a kill. Like African wild dogs and hyenas, wolves hunt in packs, using teamwork, stamina and speed to track prey.

- **Location: North America and Eurasia**
- **Habitat: mountains, forests and tundra**
- **Length: 1.5m**

Amphibians

The brightly coloured skin of the golden poison-dart frog warns of toxins that can kill in seconds. The poison is a defence against predators.

- **Location: Colombia, South America**
- **Habitat: rainforest**
- **Length: 5cm**

Spiders

A Sydney funnel web spider prepares to strike. Efficient killers, spiders inject venom through their fangs to paralyze or kill prey.

- **Location: eastern Australia**
- **Habitat: forested uplands**
- **Body length: 3.5cm**

Snakes

As a gaboon viper bites into a mouse, venom pumps out of its fangs. Not all snakes use venom to kill. Constrictors coil their body around their victim, hugging it to death.

- **Location: sub-Saharan Africa**
- **Habitat: rainforest and savannah**
- **Length: 1.5m**

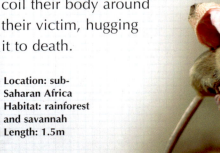

http://video.nationalgeographic.com/video/worlds-deadliest

DEFENCE – to protect someone or something from attack

ATTACK AND DEFENCE

Mammals are successful because they are very adaptable. Some predators, such as lions, work together to take down prey, while others, including tigers, are lone hunters. Camouflage (blending into the background) is a great defence against predators. Herds provide protection for weaker members – musk oxen form defensive rings round their young when threatened.

"The scientific name of an animal that doesn't either run from or fight its enemies is lunch."

Michael Friedman (born 1960)
American poet

Best defence
When a wolf snarls, it is a terrifying sight – enough to make most attackers take to their heels. By displaying their teeth in this way, wolves have found a very effective method of defence.

Distracting patterns
The black and white markings on a zebra are unique to that individual animal. When a herd of zebra is moving together it is hard for a predator, such as a crocodile, to make out where one animal ends and another begins. This patterning is called disruptive coloration, and it is a superb defence.

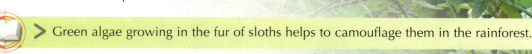

> Green algae growing in the fur of sloths helps to camouflage them in the rainforest.

☻ ARMOURED BALL

When threatened, an armadillo – Spanish for 'little armoured one' – rolls up into a ball. Its soft underside is protected by the bony, skin-covered armour on the top of its body and tail. Pangolins protect themselves in a similar fashion, their upper bodies covered by overlapping scales. The hedgehog, by contrast, has spines all over its back and sides, and forms a prickly ball.

three-banded armadillo

hinged back allows flexibility

defensive ball is impenetrable

http://mentalfloss.com/article/12258/7-absolutely-insane-animal-defense-mechanisms

Hunting as a team

The chimpanzees that live in the forests of West Africa eat fruit, leaves and nuts, but they also hunt monkeys. The monkeys are smaller and able to leap onto branches that would break under the chimpanzees' weight. The male hunters have found that they can catch their prey by working as a team.

KEY

1 **Red colobus monkeys**

2 **Driver chimpanzee at rear makes sure monkeys keep moving**

3 **Clearly visible blocker prevents monkeys changing direction**

4 **Second blocker hoots and screams, cutting off escape**

5 **Chaser joins in the hunt**

6 **Second chaser rushes up a tree to join in**

7 **Ambusher anticipates where the monkeys will move to, only showing himself at the last minute**

HUNTING SKILLS

There are no more expert hunters than the birds of prey. They hunt from the air, using their keen senses of sight and hearing to target prey – eagles can spot a moving rabbit at a distance of three kilometres. Peregrines stoop at an incredible 320 kilometres per hour, striking with sharp talons and killing by impact. The nocturnal barn owl is able to find its mouse prey in complete darkness.

wingspan of up to 1.7m

secondary flight feathers give the bird lift

Powerful scavenger
Like vultures, Marabou storks have naked heads and necks, adaptations for scavenging. These large birds are up to 1.4m high and weigh up to 8kg. They seek out all kinds of prey, both alive and dead, and if their heads were covered in feathers, it would be difficult to keep them clean.

Absolute control
The smaller a hummingbird is, the faster its wings beat. When a 10cm-long buff-bellied hummingbird sips nectar from a flower, its wings beat at an amazing 40 times per second. These birds' wings allow them to fly forwards, up and down, sideways and backwards.

Hummingbirds have such control that they can hover on the spot.

> The Australian pelican has the longest beak at up to 47cm.

barbule†

barb

Closely linked barbs and barbules form a smooth surface for flight.

Flight feathers are long and stiff, giving the bird lift and allowing it to manoeuvre.

primary feathers propel the bird through the air

The Eurasian kingfisher has dazzling blue and orange plumage.

strongly curved beak used to tear fish apart

Snatching prey

The poise and control of the hunting bird can be seen clearly when the magnificent osprey catches its favourite fish food. It flies low over the water's surface, then plunges feet-first, sometimes right into the water, its talons outstretched to snatch up a fish.

Diving for food

Kingfishers have a dramatic hunting method. They sit still on a branch above a stream, waiting for signs of movement. Then they dive swiftly and steeply into the water, capturing the fish in their dagger-shaped beak at a depth of no more than 25cm. They beat their wings to resurface, returning to their perch to eat their prey.

⊖ BEAK SHAPES

All birds have beaks that are specially adapted to find the food that will enable them to survive in a particular environment. For example, some have hard tips to kill prey or crack nuts, while others have sensitive tips to locate food by touch.

A parrot's strong, curved beak breaks into nuts and fruit to extract the seeds.

A pelican dives, using its pouch as a fishing net. It tips its beak to drain the water then eats the fish whole.

The flamingo swings its upside-down beak from side to side in water, filtering out small food items.

HUNTERS AND PREY

Many people think the rainforests are alive with fierce, meat-eating animals. Yet there are few large rainforest predators, and they are hard to spot. Hunters have to stay hidden, or their prey will see them. Leopards, jaguars and other cats climb trees in search of food, or lie in wait in the undergrowth. Other fearsome killers live on the forest floor. Snakes hide in the litter of leaves and twigs, catching rodents, frogs and even deer.

Top cats

Cats live in the understorey of the rainforests. These are some of the biggest and strongest of all jungle animals. Scientists call them 'top predators' because they have no natural enemies to fear. The clouded leopard hunts monkeys and squirrels, which it swipes to the ground with its paws. The jaguar ambushes deer and other game animals by leaping unseen from the ground onto their backs.

KILLERS IN CAMOUFLAGE

Camouflage is a way of deceiving the eye. Different colours or shapes allow animals to blend in with the surroundings so it is hard to see them. This is vital for cats and other predators that ambush their prey. Leopards and jaguars have dark spots on their fur, and others have stripes. These break up the shape of a cat's body. Smaller creatures, such as insects, also use camouflage to hide from their enemies. Most species of mantis are shaped and coloured to look just like leaves.

frock-coated mantis camouflaged on leaf

massive paws and sharp claws used to catch prey

Death from above

The king vulture lives high in the canopy. It finds prey by using its keen sense of smell, swooping on mammals or fish. Like other vultures, the king vulture scavenges on dead creatures with its powerful beak.

spotted coat mimics the dappled shade of the undergrowth

 A fully grown jaguar needs to catch one wild peccary (a pig-like animal) each week to stay alive.

The jaguar has the most powerful jaw muscles of all cats.

large ears pick up the slightest sound

four large canine teeth help to grip prey tightly

http://worldwildlife.org/species/jaguar

Poison pump

The bushmaster snake of South America grows to more than 3m long. It has heat sensors on its head that detect warmth from other animals. Once it has caught the prey in its jaws, the bushmaster injects deadly poison through its fangs.

INVESTIGATE

Encounter killer creatures for yourself in zoos, safari parks and museum exhibits, or find out more on the page or online.

bald eagle diving after prey

Zoos and safari parks

Visit a zoo or safari park to get up close to a range of predators, and to find out about breeding programmes and other conservation measures to protect animals in the wild.

 The Truth about the Most Dangerous Creatures on Earth by Nicola Davies (Walker)

 Africa Alive! Whites Lane, Kessingland, Lowestoft, Suffolk, NR33 7TF, UK

www.wellingtonzoo.com

poison dart frog

Books and magazines

If you enjoy absorbing facts and looking at amazing photographs, check out some of the many information books and magazines about dangerous creatures.

 Navigators: Killer Creatures by Claire Llewellyn (Kingfisher)

 Wildlife Photographer of the Year exhibition, Natural History Museum, Cromwell Road, London SW7 5BD, UK

 www.discoverwildlife.com

trapdoor spider about to attack

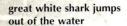

Museums and exhibitions

Visit the many museums and special exhibitions that have interactive displays and give expert information to visitors about all kinds of animals.

great white shark jumps out of the water

 World's Deadliest Animals by Matt Roper (Summersdale)

 National Museum of Scotland, Chambers Street, Edinburgh, EH1 1JF, UK

www.museum.manchester.ac.uk/kids/amazingfacts

Documentaries and movies

There are lots of animal documentaries on television and movies at the cinema that will take you right into the world of your favourite killer creatures.

 Big Cat Diary: Cheetah by Jonathan Scott and Angela Scott (Collins)

 IMAX 3D cinema, Science Museum, Exhibition Road, London, SW7 2DD, UK

 www.bbc.co.uk/nature/wildlife

LAND
KILLERS

BIG CATS

Long claws, dagger-like teeth and powerful, crushing jaws – big cats have plenty of weapons. Add to these their sharp senses, stealth, speed and power and you have one of the animal world's top killers. Most big cats are lone hunters, stalking their prey slowly and silently, then sprinting forwards to pounce and deliver the killer bite.

A lioness closes in on a young kudu antelope.

Climbing cats

Leopards drag antelope and other kills up trees, out of the way of scavengers. Like all big cats, leopards use their fang-like canines to grasp a victim around the throat, choking it to death.

Teamwork

The lion is the only big cat that lives and hunts in groups. Fleet-footed lionesses do most of the hunting. Step by step, they approach their prey – a herd of antelope, wildebeest or zebra. Suddenly, one lioness breaks cover to make a kill while the others lend support from the side.

http://bigcatswildcats.com

Killer jaws

Cats use their jagged carnassial teeth, which slice against one another like scissors, to cut up their kill. Small front teeth called incisors nibble flesh from the bone.

A feeding tiger defends its kill.

Living in a pride

Hunting together allows lions to bring down larger prey, providing food for the whole pride. The males protect the kill from hungry scavengers, giving the cubs more time to eat their fill.

"So have I heard on
Africa's burning shore,
A hungry lion give a grievous roar."

William Barnes Rhodes (1772–1826)
from the opera Bombastes Furioso, *1810*

Night vision

Most cats hunt at night. At the back of their eyes is a golden layer, the tapetum, which shines when caught in a light. It helps the eyes to absorb extra light, boosting the cat's night vision.

DEADLY SPRINTER

A cheetah, the fastest animal on land, accelerates faster than most cars, reaching a top speed of 95km/h in 3–4 seconds. Unlike the other big cats, a cheetah cannot retract, or pull back, its claws inside its paws. Instead, the claws work like the spikes on a sprinter's shoes, helping the cheetah to grip the ground. The life-or-death chase across the grasslands is usually over in 20 seconds.

lightweight body with long, thin and muscular legs

Flexible spine powers huge bounds of up to 7m.

⊖ CRUSHING JAWS

Hyenas have massive jaws filled with strong teeth. Their sharp canine teeth tear at a victim's skin, while the molars are so powerful that they can chew through a zebra's thigh bone to reach the tasty marrow inside.

temporalis muscle

masseter muscle

canine

molar

A spotted hyena carries its kill – a disembowelled impala

PACK HUNTERS

Hyenas hunt in packs, which helps them to bring down large prey such as antelope and zebra. These fearless, fast and lightly-built hunters pursue their prey over long distances, taking turns to lead the pack so no individual gets too tired. Other pack hunters include Australian dingoes and African wild dogs.

> Four out of every five attacks by African wild dogs end in a successful kill.

African wild dog

A female spotted hyena faces up to a pair of snarling African wild dogs.

Bad neighbours

Both hyenas and wild dogs live on the savannah grasslands of Africa. Packs of hyenas will charge wild dogs in an attempt to steal their feast. Who wins will depend on speed, aggression and the number of animals in each pack.

Dog meat

Once an animal has been caught by a pack of wild dogs, it is ripped apart. The dogs bolt down their kill before hyenas, lions and vultures move in to pick at the remains.

Night prowlers

The hyena looks like a dog but belongs to a different animal family. Hyenas are efficient scavengers and skilful predators. They hunt by night in small groups, killing much larger prey. With strong jaws and powerful digestive systems, they can eat and extract goodness even from their victims' teeth and bones.

"Hyenas are larger and stronger, but wild dogs attack in formation, like a crack squad of commandos."

Steve Leonard (born 1972)
British wildlife presenter and writer

Dingoes kill kangaroos, wallabies and smaller prey, such as this monitor lizard.

Wild dog down under

Australian dingoes are descended from wolf-like dogs. They have been known to attack children, so in dingo country parents need to be aware of this danger.

WOLVES OF THE TAIGA

TAIGA – *coniferous forest stretching across Asia, northern Europe and North America*

Wolves live and hunt in a pack, up to 30 animals strong. As soon as the pack detects prey – perhaps a herd of caribou or elk – it gives chase, zoning in on any animal that lags behind. Sharp teeth snap at the victim's heels, slowing it down so that other pack members can get a grip. When prey is brought down, the wolves rip at its flesh. For large victims, such as elk, death is often slow.

Feeding time

Wolf packs share their food but there is a strict pecking order. First to feed are the pack leaders – the alpha male and female. Once they give the signal, the rest of the pack can join in. The wolves devour the kill, crushing bones to reach the rich, fatty marrow and leaving little waste.

Wolves are intelligent animals and use calls and physical gestures to communicate with one another.

prey animal

Low head, low ears, low tail – this wolf is under pressure!

2.5cm-long canines grasp and rip prey.

Eyes give sharp, binocular vision.

 > A wolf needs an average of 1.5kg of meat a day. A large kill such as a bison will last a pack of wolves a week.

www.defenders.org/gray-wolf/basic-facts

Bear trouble

Grey wolves in Alaska, USA, attempt to defend their kill from a hungry grizzly bear. Wolves and bears make uneasy neighbours. Bears are big and dangerous but wolf packs can snatch and kill young bear cubs.

STAMINA AND SPEED

Wolves are muscular and, during a chase, can reach a top speed of 56km/h. At other times, wolves prefer to trot, their long, strong legs covering one metre with each and every stride. They can keep up this pace for hours, covering 100km in a single night.

Each wolf runs in the footprints made by the leader.

Large front feet help to prevent a wolf from sinking in soft snow.

"The aim of life was meat. Life itself was meat. Life lived on life. There were the eaters and the eaten. The law was: EAT OR BE EATEN."

Jack London (1876–1916)
from the novel White Fang, *1906*

Long hair makes the wolf look larger.

Sensitive ears hear prey up to 16km away.

Nose detects prey up to 2km away.

Pack discipline

A strict social order in the pack prevents scuffles from escalating into fights. Youngsters give way to older animals and the weak submit to the strong. All pups develop strength and hunting skills through play fights such as these.

ARCTIC GIANTS

The largest of all land carnivores, polar bears are also at home in the sea, where their size, power and swimming ability allow them to catch walruses and whales. More commonly, the bears hunt ringed seals at their breathing holes. When a bear senses an approaching seal, it punches the ice with its paw, grabs the seal's head in its jaws and yanks the body on to the ice.

cross-section through hair, shown 350 times bigger than life size

Long outer hairs are hollow, which traps warm air close to the bear's body.

"Something in the bear's presence made [Lyra] feel close to coldness, danger, brutal power…"

Philip Pullman (born 1946)
from the novel Northern Lights, *1995*

Bear legs

On thin ice, the polar bear's massive feet help to spread its weight over a large area. In water, the paws act as paddles. Polar bears swim with their front legs, stretching out their back legs to work as a rudder.

Learning to hunt

After killing a seal, a polar bear rips open the carcass and, with her cub, feeds on the meat and blubber. Later, the bears will roll in the snow to clean their coats of blood. Females teach their cubs the art of stalking seals, but many attempts fail as the cubs fidget and give the game away.

Out at sea

Polar bears are supreme swimmers and have been seen 100km from land, still powering through the water. In pursuit of prey, they can dive as deep as 4.5m and stay below the surface for more than a minute.

 > A large male polar bear on its hind feet stands over 3m tall and weighs more than nine men.

Big, brown bear

Grizzly bears are found in the frozen regions of Russia and North America. These formidable hunters kill prey as large as moose but also catch fish and dig out burrowing creatures, such as ground squirrels.

Strong jaws and a variety of teeth allow grizzlies to feed on any food.

The powerful front paws are equipped with claws up to 15cm long.

Beluga whale's tail thrashes wildly.

short, curved claws for grabbing prey,

white beluga whale, a rare catch for a polar bear

🔴 NOSY NEIGHBOUR

Polar bears are not usually man-eaters, but hungry ones can pose a dangerous threat. A television cameraman once came face to face with a bear through the window of his cabin. He fired a flare gun to scare it off, but the bear came back – twice. On nights like that it must be hard to sleep!

Feet pads (and nose) are the only furless body parts.

INVESTIGATE

Find out how the experts know about land animals, and explore their natural world by checking out safari parks, museums, books and websites.

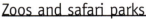

Zoos and safari parks

Take a trip to a safari park or zoo and experience encounters with killer creatures first hand and face to face.

male leopard hunting in Kenya

 My Big Cats Journal by Steve Bloom (Thames & Hudson)

 Taronga Western Plains Zoo, Obley Road, Dubbo, New South Wales, 2830, Australia

 www.woburnsafari.co.uk

wolf howling

Books and magazines

You can become an expert on predators by reading information books and magazines about these animals.

 25 Most Deadly Animals in the World, by IIC Wildlife (Amazon Kindle)

 Subscribe to a magazine, such as Eco Kids Planet, www.ecokidsplanet.co.uk, to receive new information about animals every month.

spotted hyena

 www.animalfactguide.com

Museums and exhibitions

Visit museums and exhibitions to get to know more about animals in the wild and how they interact with their environment.

 The Natural History Museum Book of Predators, by Steve Parker (Natural History Museum)

 Horniman Museum, 100 London Road, Forest Hill, London, SE23 3PQ, UK

 http://www.kidsplanet.org/factsheets/map.html

polar bear on drift ice feeding on a seal in Svalbard, Norway

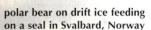

Documentaries and movies

Watching movies and documentaries can be a really exciting way to see animals in action.

 Africa (BBC Films)

 Enter into any creature's natural habitat in your own home by searching for animal clips on the Internet.

 www.bbc.co.uk/newsround/animals

OCEAN KILLERS

VIBRATION – *a rippling movement through air or water*

SAVAGE SHARKS

If any animal has the reputation of 'killer creature', it is the shark. Sleek and efficient predators with tiptop senses and massive jaws, sharks hunt prey as large as elephant seals and squid. Some sharks circle their prey and disable it before killing. Others attack by surprise from below.

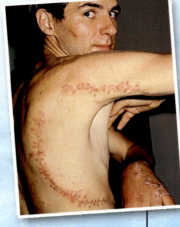

"What we are dealing with here is a perfect engine, an eating machine."

Matt Hooper
fictional marine biologist in the film Jaws, 1975

Man-eater?

A survivor of a great white shark attack displays his stitches. Great whites are more feared than any other creature in the sea – and with good reason. They carry out more attacks than any other kind of shark.

Shark senses

Sharks use many senses to find their prey. They detect vibrations (movement) and even faint trails of blood from wounded creatures. They also sense the weak electrical signals given out by all living things.

skin pore

The ampullae of Lorenzini are sense organs on a shark's snout that detect electrical signals.

scalloped hammerhead shark

sea lion

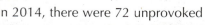

In 2014, there were 72 unprovoked shark attacks on humans.

Gills take in oxygen from the water.

● TEETH

A shark's jaws are lined with rows of teeth. Some species have long, narrow, needle-like teeth for impaling fish and other small prey. Those that feed on larger animals have broad, serrated teeth to tear off chunks of flesh. Like disposable razor blades, shark teeth have a short life and are replaced as they break or wear out.

serrated edge for cutting

muscular tail fin

gall bladder

stomach

streamlined body

Large liver helps shark to float.

Strength and speed

A great white smashes into its prey at around 48km/h. In the split second before the impact, it lifts its snout and leads with its upper jaws. The force of the attack carries the shark out of the water with 100kg of meat in its mouth.

FEROCIOUS ORCAS

Orcas, also known as killer whales, are giants of the sea. These mammals, which are a type of dolphin, grow up to nine metres long and live in family groups called pods. Fast, fierce and intelligent hunters, orcas work together to kill prey very much bigger than themselves, such as great white sharks and humpback whales, as well as hundreds of smaller species.

Athletes of the sea

Killer whales are remarkably agile for their size. They chase and catch fast-moving penguins and fish, and even snap ducks out of the air. They toss their victims out of the water before swallowing them whole.

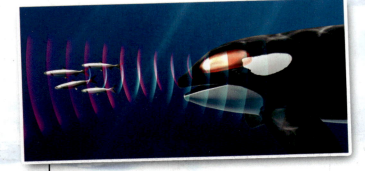

Sound hunters

Killer whales use a hunting technique called echolocation, which is especially useful in deep, murky water. They send out a stream of high-pitched clicks, then listen for the echoes that bounce back off their prey.

On the shore, sea lion pups are vulnerable and slow.

> There is no known instance of a wild orca killing a person.

Beach raider

A killer whale surfs on to a beach, where sea lion pups are playing on the shore. It seizes a pup in its huge jaws, then flops back into the water to be washed out to sea. This is a tricky manoeuvre, but the reward of sea lion meat is worth the risk of getting stranded.

"If they'd wanted to they could have tossed me and my kayak high into the air with just a flick of their tail."

Steve Leonard (born 1972)
British wildlife presenter and writer—

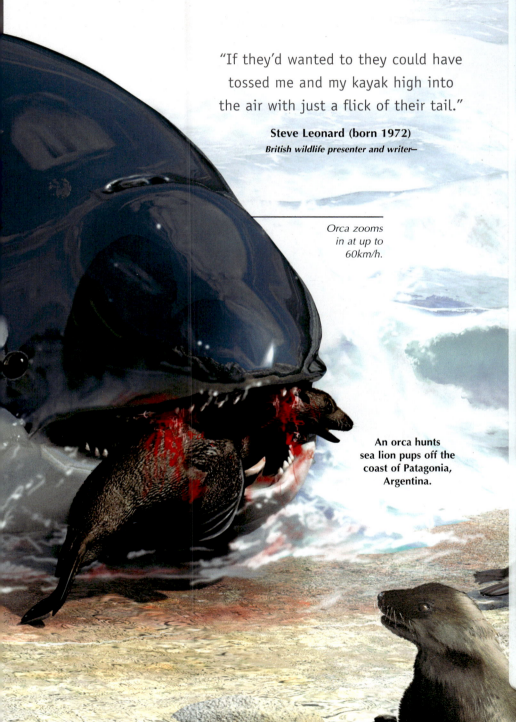

Orca zooms in at up to 60km/h.

An orca hunts sea lion pups off the coast of Patagonia, Argentina.

● MASTER HUNTERS

Killer whales are inventive hunters. As well as using echolocation to find prey, they also make use of other techniques, including herding and trapping. They employ different methods for different types of prey.

Orcas herd shoals of herring into a tight ball, then slap them with their powerful tails to stun individuals.

After separating a whale calf from its mother, three orcas block off its route up to the surface to breathe.

While staking out a seal hidden in an underwater cave, these orcas hunt and breathe in relay.

Orcas head-butt ice floes to tip off penguins and seals, or whip up the water with their tails to wash them off.

http://seaworld.org/en/animal-infobooks/killer-whale/habitat-and-distribution

PREDATORY PIRANHAS

Piranhas are small freshwater fish that live in the rivers of South America. They have strong, upturned jaws like those of a bulldog, and remarkably sharp teeth. Not all species of piranha are aggressive, but those that are have a fearsome reputation. When they are hungry and gang up in a school, they work together as one ferocious killing machine, targeting birds, rodents, frogs and young caimans.

Caught by a caiman
A shoal of 20–30 piranhas may be a threat to a young caiman, but this lone fish stands no chance against a fully grown black caiman.

An excited piranha turns on another. Even though these fish hunt together, within the shoal it is every fish for itself.

 KILLER JAWS

A piranha's upper and lower teeth fit together so neatly that they can remove a perfect, crescent-shaped chunk of flesh. Amazonian Indians have used the razor-sharp teeth for sharpening darts, shaving and cutting.

In the dry season, piranhas can be stranded in small lakes with little food. This makes them more aggressive.

jaw packed with triangular teeth

 > In Brazil about 1,200 cattle are killed by piranhas every year.

Feeding frenzy

A young heron has fallen from its treetop nest into the river. Within seconds, its struggles have alerted a shoal of red-bellied piranhas. Smaller fish size up the prey, taking a few test bites before larger piranhas drag the bird below the surface.

www.extremescience.com/piranha.htm

Nostrils can detect a single drop of blood in 200 litres of water.

STINGERS IN THE SEA

In the warm, clear waters off northern Australia lies the Great Barrier Reef, the world's largest system of coral reefs. Built by the skeletons of tiny coral polyps, it stretches for more than 2,000 kilometres. The reef supports an astonishing variety of life, including more than 400 different corals. But, divers beware! Lurking in these blue waters are some of the deadliest creatures in the sea.

"In Australia, jellyfish season kicks off in November... Swarms of 3,500–4,000 jellyfish are not uncommon."

Steve Leonard (born 1972)
British wildlife presenter and writer

Blue-ringed octopus
With a body just the size of a golf ball, the blue-ringed octopus contains enough poison to kill ten people. The danger lies in the bite from its parrot-like beak, which is sharp enough to pierce a diver's wetsuit.

DEATH BY STINGRAY

Stingrays have venomous spines on the end of their tail for protection. Steve Irwin, the Australian conservationist, was killed in 2006 when a stingray whipped its tail barb into his chest and damaged his heart.

diver with southern stingray

 > The largest stingrays are 1.8m wide and 4.2m long, including their tail.

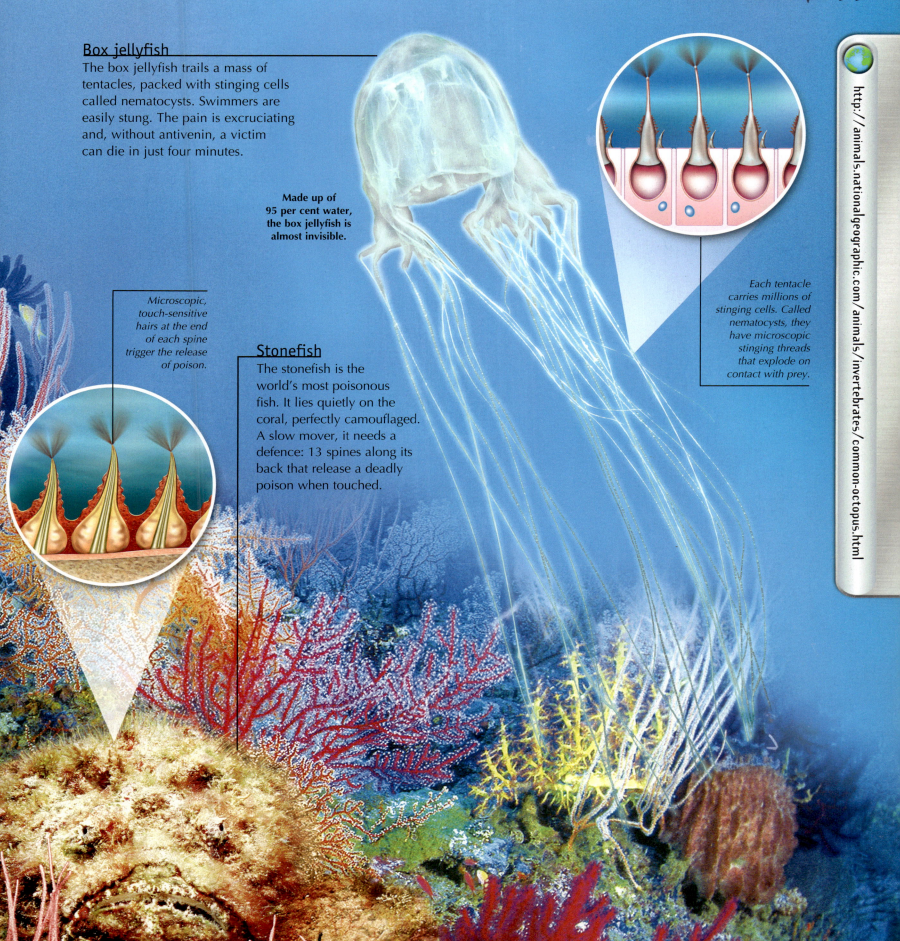

Box jellyfish

The box jellyfish trails a mass of tentacles, packed with stinging cells called nematocysts. Swimmers are easily stung. The pain is excruciating and, without antivenin, a victim can die in just four minutes.

Made up of 95 per cent water, the box jellyfish is almost invisible.

Each tentacle carries millions of stinging cells. Called nematocysts, they have microscopic stinging threads that explode on contact with prey.

Microscopic, touch-sensitive hairs at the end of each spine trigger the release of poison.

Stonefish

The stonefish is the world's most poisonous fish. It lies quietly on the coral, perfectly camouflaged. A slow mover, it needs a defence: 13 spines along its back that release a deadly poison when touched.

http://animals.nationalgeographic.com/animals/invertebrates/common-octopus.html

IN THE DEEP

Light does not penetrate beyond a few hundred metres below the surface of Earth's oceans. In these dark and hostile waters live some of the strangest creatures on the planet. Many of them are fierce predators, with sharp teeth, flexible jaws and unusual hunting strategies. Living at great depths, they are seldom seen and little is known about their life cycles.

> **PHOTOPHORE** – a light-producing organ found in some deep-sea fish

A 60cm-long female bearded anglerfish, or illuminated netdevil, floats motionless. The bioluminescent lure on its head and barbel (beard) hanging from its chin attract prey towards its gaping jaws.

anglerfish can move and light up their lures when needed

elaborate barbel resembles a piece of seaweed, attracting shrimps and other prey

When the tiny 6mm-long male bearded anglerfish finds a female, he bites into her skin and fuses with her, becoming part of her body. This means that, when she is ready to spawn, there is a mate immediately available.

Light in the darkness

Deep-sea fish have adapted in many varied ways to the different depths at which they live. Some species have special organs called photophores that give off bioluminescent light – a light produced by a chemical reaction. Other species have 'fishing-rods' that act as lures, or long feelers that help them seek out prey.

circular photophores behind each eye illuminate the water with a red glow

The stoplight loosejaw dragonfish is unusual – it can produce and see red light. In depths of up to 2,500m, it also produces green light from a comma-shaped photophore beneath each eye.

The living fossil

In 1938, an unusual fish was caught in the western Indian Ocean. It was identified as a coelacanth, which was thought to have been extinct for at least 65 million years. Coelacanths can be up to 2m long and live at depths of up to 700m.

underside is covered in glowing photophores

The cookiecutter shark has been found in water up to 3,500m below the surface. This small shark attaches itself to prey such as a whale and spins to cut out a cookie-shaped plug of flesh.

Deep-sea shark

This rarely seen frilled shark looks more like an eel than a shark. It has 300 distinctive pronged teeth and an extraordinary curved tail fin. It is up to 2m long and hunts fish, squid and other sharks at depths of up to 1,500m. This species has changed very little since prehistoric times.

third 'leg' formed from extended tail fin

The tripodfish lives at the bottom of the ocean. To catch prey, it 'stands' on the sea floor, facing into the current and waiting for small crustaceans to be swept towards it.

front 'legs' formed from extended pelvic fins

∨ The black seadevil anglerfish is the size of a tennis ball.

INVESTIGATE

Find out more about the killers of the ocean by visiting aquariums, museums and wildlife parks or finding out more in books or on the Internet.

blue-ringed octopus

Aquariums and zoos

There are lots of opportunities to come face to face with a shark or a piranha in an aquarium or zoo. Some even offer swimming with sharks experiences!

 Weird Sea Creatures by Laura Marsh (National Geographic Society)

 National Aquarium of New Zealand, Marine Parade, Napier, New Zealand

www.sharktrust.co.uk/en/shark_factsheets

great white shark

Books and magazines

Libraries are great places to find out all sorts of strange and interesting facts about deep sea creatures and ocean predators.

 Dangerous Animals of the Sea by Samantha Flores (Amazon)

 Zoo and aquarium bookstores often have interesting and specialist books to buy on the creatures you have seen there.

http://ocean.nationalgeographic.com/ocean/photos/dangerous-sea-creatures

Museums and exhibitions

Many museums have amazing exhibits where you can see just how big sea creatures are in real life by standing next to them.

 Creatures of the Deep by John Woodward (Natural History Museum)

Shark Walk and Shark Valley, SeaLife Sydney Aquarium, 1–5 Wheat Road, Sydney, New South Wales, Australia

www.bristolzoo.org.uk/fish

the deadly teeth of a black piranha

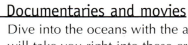

stingrays have a barbed stinger on the end of their tail

Documentaries and movies

Dive into the oceans with the amazing documentaries and films which will take you right into these creatures worlds – without even getting wet.

 Blue Planet (BBC Films)

 Watch some rare film of a black sea devil anglerfish: http://news.nationalgeographic.com/news/2014/11/141125-sea-devil-deep-sea-fish-animals-science

 http://animals.nationalgeographic.com/animals/fish

REPTILES AND
AMPHIBIANS

REPTILE SENSES

"Use your enemy's hand
to catch a snake."

Persian proverb

Most reptiles are skilled at spotting moving prey. There are some, such as blind snakes, that have only poor eyesight because they live underground. Snakes do not have an ear opening and can only hear very low sounds, feeling sound through their bodies as they slither along. Many reptiles use their tongue to touch, and some snakes use it to taste.

brain

nerve

forked tongue

Jacobson's organ

The viper's forked tongue rubs off the scents it has collected onto the Jacobson's organ in the roof of the mouth. The organ analyzes the scents and sends a message to the brain.

A slender anole is quite unaware of the danger it is in. One lunge by the viper and it is all over.

The deeper the fork in the tongue, the more the Jacobson's organ is used.

> Special ligaments in a snake's jaw allow it to swallow prey many times bigger than the size of its head.

http://faculty.washington.edu/chudler/amaze.html

The eyelash pit viper uses its strong, prehensile tail to grip onto the branch as it launches its body through the air towards its prey.

Sensing food

An eyelash pit viper – so-called because of the spiny scales over each eye – strikes, its mouth open to give a venomous bite. The forked tongue, flicking in and out and tasting the air, has detected the scent of potential prey. On the front of its face, heat sensors called pits have indicated the exact location and size of the anole lizard.

Hunting with a lure

There are two red structures on the tip of an alligator snapping turtle's tongue. These wriggle like small worms, acting as a lure for swimming prey. All this North American turtle has to do is sit on the bottom of a river with its mouth open and wait for a fish to swim in.

🕑 A THIRD EYE

New Zealand's tuataras are called 'living fossils' because they have hardly changed in 200 million years. They have a tiny third 'eye' on the top of the head. It is visible in hatchlings, but is then covered with scales. The eye is connected to the pineal gland and may, by interpreting the amount of light falling on it, trigger sleep and hibernation.

Scary senses

A snake can sense vibrations through the ground, alerting it to nearby prey. It also picks up scents with its tongue. The tongue wipes airborne particles on to the roof of the mouth, where special cells send messages to the snake's brain that allow it to identify the scent.

Diamondback rattlesnake is named for its diamond-shaped markings.

Tail rattle makes sound to warn off predators.

VENOMOUS SNAKES

With its slithering body and lightning speed, the snake is one of the most feared hunters. Many venomous snakes lie in wait for prey. When a victim comes near, the snake rears up and strikes, injecting lethal venom from its fangs. Venom is a clever means of attack, hijacking dangerous prey with little physical contact. The poison paralyzes or kills quickly, and may even begin to break down the body for digestion.

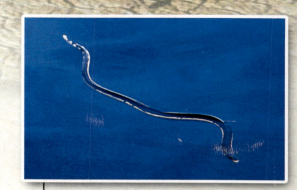

Sea snakes

Found in tropical waters, sea snakes are among the most poisonous reptiles. Luckily, they rarely come into contact with people and are not aggressive. One exception is the beaked sea snake of Australia. It carries out 90 per cent of fatal sea snake attacks.

 > Australia is home to 11 of the top 12 most venomous land snakes.

Spraying venom

As well as injecting prey, a cobra spits venom to defend itself. It can hit an enemy's eyes from as far away as 2.4m, causing temporary blindness.

Snake detects smells with its nostrils, as well as with the cells of the Jacobson's organ in the mouth.

🔴 CAMOUFLAGED KILLERS

With no limbs, many snakes cannot chase prey. Instead, they wait for prey to come to them. They have such excellent camouflage that they are almost impossible to see, especially as they keep so still. Depending on their habitat, snakes have colours and markings that blend in with leaves, vines, sand or rock.

A gaboon viper's markings resemble leaf litter.

Venom

Special glands produce the venom, which is squeezed along tiny tubes into the hollow fangs. The venom is forced through tiny openings in the fangs and injected into puncture wounds made by the sharp fang tips.

collared lizard

Forked tongue collects scent particles from the air as it flicks to and fro.

"When you see a rattlesnake poised to strike you, do not wait until he has struck before you crush him."

Franklin D. Roosevelt (1882–1945)
US President, 1933–1945

CONSTRICTOR CRUSH

Constrictors, such as boas, pythons and anacondas, kill with power not poison. When these snakes strike, they rapidly throw muscular coils around their prey's body. Each time the victim breathes out, the coils tighten a little more, so that it cannot breathe in. The tight squeeze also stops the prey's blood flowing. Unable to pump blood, the heart comes to a fatal standstill.

South American giant

The anaconda is the world's heaviest snake, weighing 200kg or more. It lives in or near water, catching capybaras and other animals that come to drink, as well as river turtles and caimans.

young red-tail boa constricting a mouse

A mouse's fate

While suffocating its prey, a boa constrictor keeps a firm grip with sharp, hooked teeth. These teeth are no use for chewing, though, so the boa must swallow its victim whole.

● EXPLODING PYTHON

In 2005, in Everglades National Park in Florida, USA, the remains of an alligator were found sticking out of a dead Burmese python. The snake's stomach had been ripped open by the alligator's claws.

alligator's tail

burst stomach

python's tail

> The reticulated python is the world's longest snake. It can grow up to 9m long.

Backwards-facing teeth drag in food.

breathing tube

jaws joined by stretchy ligaments

Stretchy jaws

A snake's jaws are joined by ligaments that stretch to give it the necessary gape to eat its super-sized meals. The snake can breathe with its mouth full because it has a movable breathing tube at the front of the lower jaw.

Constrictor's ribs can move apart to make room for swallowed prey.

"None of them knew the limits of [Kaa the python's] power, none of them could look him in the face, and none had ever come alive out of his hug."

Rudyard Kipling (1865–1936)
from the novel The Jungle Book, *1894*

Down in one

A boa usually swallows prey headfirst, so the legs do not get stuck in its throat. The snake coats its dinner with slippery saliva, then uses strong muscles to push the food into its stomach. Here, powerful juices dissolve the flesh and bones.

http://animals.nationalgeographic.com/animals/reptiles/boa-constrictor.html

DANGEROUS AMPHIBIANS

The world's most poisonous animal is a small amphibian from the rainforests of Colombia. To deter predators, the golden poison-dart frog has deadly toxins in its skin that attack the nervous system, rapidly causing heart failure. The cane toad is another amphibian that produces poisons in its skin for self defence.

NERVOUS SYSTEM – the brain, spinal cord and nerves, which collect and respond to information about the state of the body

Poisonous toad

The cane toad, a native of Central and South America, is seriously poisonous. Glands on its shoulders produce a milky poison, containing a deadly cocktail of 14 chemicals that cause convulsions and death. Introduced into Australia in the 1930s to control insect pests, the 2kg toad is now poisoning rare native species.

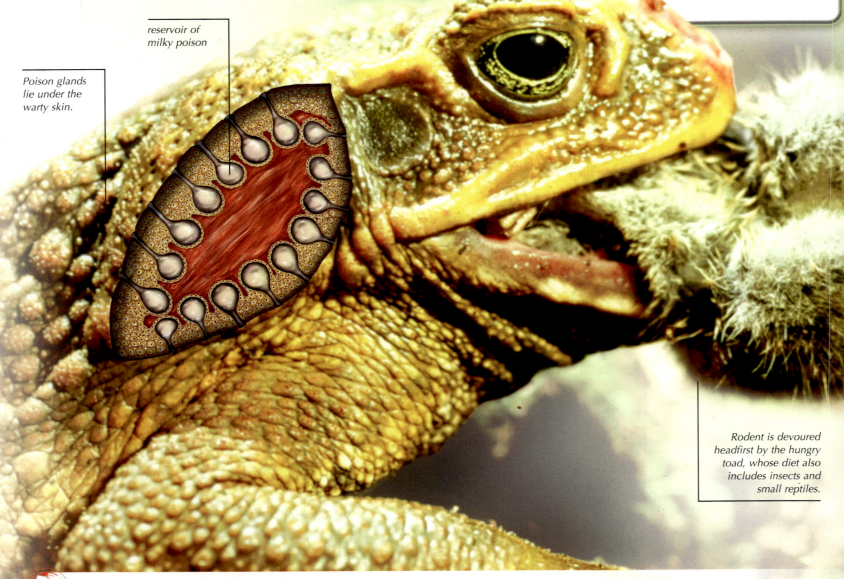

reservoir of milky poison

Poison glands lie under the warty skin.

Rodent is devoured headfirst by the hungry toad, whose diet also includes insects and small reptiles.

Poison-dart frogs get their name because the Chocó people of Central America rub the poison on the darts they use for hunting.

Ant's body contains poisons – if a frog preys on the ant, the poisons transfer to the frog.

Deadly diet

A poison-dart frog's poison comes from its diet of ants, termites, beetles and centipedes. These minibeasts absorb poisonous chemicals from the plants they eat. Frogs that are moved to a zoo lose their toxicity because they are not eating their natural diet.

Cane toads hunt at night. They locate prey by noticing movement or by tracking their scent.

Colour code

In daylight hours this poison-dart frog is protected by its colours and pattern, which warn other animals that it is best left alone. After dark, predators such as this tarantula are warned off by the taste of the frog's skin.

http://nationalzoo.si.edu/Animals/Amazonia/Facts/fact-poisondartfrog.cfm

green poison-dart frog and tarantula

golden poison-dart frog

"Even crocodiles have been found dead with cane toads in their mouths."

Mary Summerill (born 1958)
Presenter of the BBC documentary series
Wild Down Under, *2003*

🔴 HOW TOXIC ARE THEY?

A golden poison-dart frog is just 5cm long, but its body contains enough poison to kill 10 humans – or an astonishing 25,000 mice. How does that compare with other poisonous creatures?

Golden poison-dart frog could kill 25,000 mice.

Black widow spider could kill 700 mice.

King cobra could kill 3,500 mice.

Glides over distances of up to 60m have been recorded.

Flying from danger

When this tree-dwelling flying lizard is threatened, it has an unusual method of escape. It has elongated ribs with skin stretched between them, which act like wings as it glides from tree to tree. When the lizard is at rest, the ribs fold against the body.

AVOIDING PREDATORS

Reptiles have very varied ways of protecting themselves. Like other animals, they often run away, climb trees or fight back when attacked. However, many are superbly camouflaged and even able to change colour. Some lizards can shed part of their tail if seized, growing a new one in its place. Reptiles such as the frilled lizard can make themselves look bigger, and the hard shells of turtles and tortoises are an effective defence.

⊜ WARNING COLORATION

When strong contrasting colours are seen on an animal, they usually warn that the animal is dangerous. Most of the non-venomous milksnakes have bright red, black and yellow bands. These colours mimic those of the highly venomous coral snake, and the milksnake sometimes even copies the coral snake's behaviour to scare away predators.

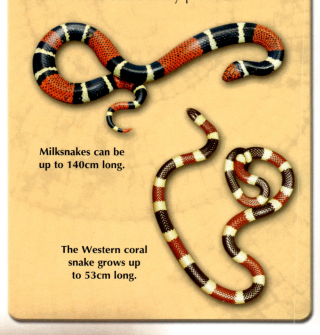

Milksnakes can be up to 140cm long.

The Western coral snake grows up to 53cm long.

A thorny problem

The thorny devil's colour changes from pale browns when warm to darker colours when cold, and this camouflage is very effective in the deserts of Australia. However, it is slow-moving and would be vulnerable to predators if it were not covered all over with sharp spines.

The thorny devil rocks backwards and forwards as it walks.

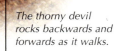

 ❯ Texas horned lizards squirt blood from ducts near their eyes at predators up to 3m away.

The distinctive curled muscular tail has adapted to grasp and balance.

Masters of disguise

Panther chameleons can be found all over the island of Madagascar, off the southeast coast of Africa. They vary in colour, and the males are generally more brightly coloured than the females. Like all chameleons, they change colour in response to changes in temperature, light or mood.

A brightly coloured adult male panther chameleon.

Chameleons are difficult to spot in leafy rainforest habitat.

"A chameleon doesn't leave one tree until he's sure of another."

Arabian proverb

Faking death

One defensive mechanism used by some animals when threatened is to play dead. A reptile that does this very effectively is the shy and elusive grass snake. It becomes completely limp, turning on its back with its mouth open and tongue lolling out.

SELF-PROTECTION

It is a dangerous world, and animals need to defend themselves. Some attack before they can be attacked. Many are armed with horns, sharp teeth, quills, claws or great strength. Some give off powerful smells or simply run away quickly, while others adopt frightening poses. Many amphibians are brightly coloured or have poisonous skin that tastes nasty to a predator. There are even toads that play dead!

> "Swallow a toad in the morning and you will encounter nothing more disgusting the rest of the day."
>
> **Nicolas de Chamfort (1741–94)**
> *French writer and wit*

Marine toads can be up to 25cm in length and over 2kg in weight.

Poisonous prey

The world's largest toad lives in the open grasslands and woodlands of Central and South America and Australia. Called the marine toad and cane toad, it is prey to snakes, caimans, birds of prey and black rats. If squeezed in their jaws, the toad oozes highly toxic fluid. However, many of its predators are immune to this poison.

Fire salamanders are nocturnal, searching for their insect prey on the forest floor at night.

Poisonous defence

The fire salamander has large glands behind its eyes and down the back on either side of the spine. If the animal is threatened, the glands produce a milky defensive chemical called salamandrin. This poison is strong enough to kill small animals.

> The 5cm-long golden poison dart frog has enough venom to kill ten grown men.

bufotoxins from glands on shoulders contain 14 chemicals

⊖ PLAYING DEAD

When threatened, the Surinam toad (above) and the Leopard frog may play dead by keeping still. The Surinam toad is particularly convincing because it is almost completely flat in shape and looks like a leaf. It also uses this ability to hunt, lying still on the bottom of streams to ambush prey.

http://animals.nationalgeographic.com/animals/amphibians/golden-poison-dart-frog.html

Poisonous frogs

The poison arrow frogs of Central and South America are protected effectively against predators such as snakes and spiders. The frogs are brilliantly coloured, and these 'warning colours' alert predators to the dangers of trying to pick them up and eat them. The frogs also secrete deadly toxins from their skin.

strawberry poison arrow frog in the rainforest

The Komodo uses its tongue to sniff out potential meals.

Saliva contains more than 60 types of bacteria.

A Komodo can weigh up to 200kg – more than two grown men.

Deadly saliva

Komodo dragons produce saliva full of harmful bacteria, which works as a primitive venom. If prey is wounded but manages to escape, it will die from the infected wound, and the dragon will find and eat it.

🔴 FATAL ATTACK

Tragically, in 2007 a Komodo killed an eight-year-old boy. The animal mauled and bit the child, shaking him viciously from side to side. His family drove off the dragon but the boy died from massive bleeding.

thick, strong neck

scaly, leathery hide

powerful limbs

LETHAL LIZARDS

Most lizards are carnivorous, but two species have serious bites that can be dangerous to humans. One is the Gila (pronounced 'heela') monster, which lives in deserts in Mexico and southwestern USA. The other is a huge monitor lizard, the Komodo dragon, whose mouth is full of deadly bacteria. The world's largest lizard, it lives on four islands in Indonesia.

  > The Komodo dragon can detect a potential meal from 5km away, using its flicking tongue to sniff the air.

Scary monster

The Gila monster is a slow-moving lizard. It tries to avoid confrontation if it can by hissing at any animals that challenge it. As a last resort, the Gila will bite, chewing to activate glands in its jaw to produce a poisonous saliva. The toxins, which flow in through the wound, cause paralysis. The Gila's eye-catching colour and skin patterns warn enemies that it is poisonous.

Dinner for six

Six Komodo dragons devour a goat. Komodos move swiftly for their size, and attack water buffaloes, boars and deer. They pin down and rip apart prey with their massive claws. Unfussy diners, Komodos eat carrion, too.

Bead-like, scaly skin is black with pink and yellow markings.

Baby rats are attacked by a Gila monster.

"The breath is very fetid and its odour can be detected at some little distance."

Scientific American **magazine, 1890**

KILLER CROCODILIANS

They look like prehistoric beasts, but crocodiles and alligators are very much alive, lurking in rivers and lakes. These reptiles are found in subtropical and tropical parts of the world, where the sun warms their cold-blooded bodies and turns them into agile hunters. The saltwater crocodile can grow as long as five metres. It devours fish, other crocodiles, birds, mammals – and unlucky humans.

Big snapper
The gharial nimbly catches fish by sweeping the water with its long, narrow snout. Its needle-like teeth are perfect for spearing slippery prey.

Deadly grip

A Nile crocodile clamps its jaws around a gazelle's neck in a Kenyan game park. Prey this large is a challenge for crocodiles because they cannot chew. They have to spin a kill until it breaks apart.

Crocodiles and alligators are believed to kill about 2,000 people every year.

Nostril is set high on the skull, so that the crocodile can breathe when hiding in water.

New teeth for old
Crocodiles have around 60 teeth. They are designed for grabbing prey rather than cutting flesh. So, to help break down large chunks of meat, crocodilians swallow stones. These churn around in one part of their stomach, grinding up the food.

Leathery skin is reinforced with bony, armoured plates called scutes.

"Don't think there are no crocodiles because the water is calm."

Malayan proverb

www.crocodilian.com

● SHOCK ATTACK

A crocodile's eyes, ears and nostrils are on the top of its head, allowing it to lie low in the water and still see, hear, smell and breathe. To save energy crocodiles wait, motionless, until a meal approaches...

Resembling a log in the river, this Nile crocodile is unseen by its prey – a zebra on its way down to drink.

The crocodile explodes out of the water in a lethal burst, clamping its jaws around the zebra's muzzle.

The terrified zebra slips on the muddy riverbank. Unable to struggle free, it is dragged into deeper water.

The crocodile spins the victim, drowning it or smashing its spine, then breaking the body into chunks.

INVESTIGATE

Get hands on with reptiles and amphibians and explore more of their natural worlds by checking out wildlife parks, books, websites and museums.

Wildlife parks and zoos

Visit a wildlife park or zoo and see some of the extraordinary variety of reptiles and amphibians that live on earth. Get close to a poisonous dart frog, a snake or a crocodile.

 100 Facts: Reptiles and Amphibians by Ann Kay (Miles Kelly)

 Amazon World Zoo Park, Isle of Wight, PO36 0LX, UK

golden dart frog

 www.australiazoo.com.au

banded sea kraits in the Bohol Sea

Books and magazines

Discover all kinds of facts about amphibians and reptiles for yourself by reading magazines and information books.

 Discover Science: Reptiles by Belinda Weber (Kingfisher)

 Visit your local library to discover a whole range of books about reptiles and amphibians.

cane toad

 http://nationalzoo.si.edu/animals/reptilesamphibians/facts

Museums and exhibitions

Natural history museums have displays and expert information about all sorts of predators, as well as stuffed specimens. Look out for themed exhibitions, too.

Australian black-headed python eating a rat

 Deadly Factbook 3: Reptiles and Amphibians by Steve Backshall (Orion)

 Natural History Museum, Cromwell Road, London SW7 5BD, UK

 www.museum.manchester.ac.uk/kids/galleries/liveanimals

Documentaries and movies

Award-winning documentaries and films allow you to watch predators displaying natural behaviour in their own habitats.

 Check out the National Geographic reptiles collection at http://video.nationalgeographic.com/video/animals/reptiles

 IMAX 3D cinema, Science Museum, Exhibition Road, South Kensington, London, SW7 2DD, UK

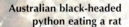 www.bbc.co.uk/nature/life/Reptile

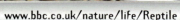

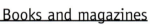

CREEPY CRAWLIES

STING OF THE SCORPION

Scorpions have stung and killed their prey for more than 400 million years – since long before the age of the dinosaurs. These ruthless and efficient hunters often eat their own weight in insects every day, grasping victims with their pincers then using their sting to inject venom. Some scorpions also spray their venom in self defence – it is hideously painful if it enters the eye.

Small but deadly

This deathstalker scorpion's venom is dangerous to people, causing pain, fever, breathing difficulties and even death. When it feels threatened, the 10cm-long deathstalker raises its tail and readies its claws to attack.

Protective poison

A scorpion mother looks after her young. She carries her brood on her back for the first few days of their lives, with her poison-tipped tail curled over them to keep enemies at bay.

🔴 HAIRY HUNTER

The rock scorpion lives in southern Africa. It hides in cracks between the rocks by day, coming out to hunt at dusk. Its fine body hairs can detect vibrations made by any nearby spiders and insects.

scorpion eating a blowfly

"Lord! how we suddenly jump, as Scorpio, or the Scorpion, stings us in the rear."

Stubb
second mate on the Pequod *in Herman Melville's* Moby Dick, 1851

 > More people die from scorpion stings each year in Mexico than in any other country.

Sting in the tail

A northern scorpion feeds on a blowfly. Scorpions range in colour from yellow and tan to brown and black. Like spiders, they belong to the arachnid family, but they store venom not in the fangs but in their muscular tail. The poison glands and sting are in the tail's last segment.

Muscles swing the sting into position and rock it to and fro.

Venom is squeezed out of the sting.

Venom is produced in tiny venom sacs.

Black widow spider

This female black widow is eating her partner after mating. Despite their name and reputation, however, black widows do not always do this. The female is far more deadly to humans. With venom 15 times deadlier than a rattlesnake's, her bite causes breathing problems and muscle cramps.

Ultra-sensitive hairs pick up sensations from the surrounding area.

"A dark leg quivered in the milk-chocolate earth, then another, and another, until the whole tarantula was revealed."

Nigel Marven (born 1960)
British wildlife presenter and writer

DEADLY ARACHNIDS

Spiders use venom to paralyze or kill their prey. The venom is made in the poison glands, then squeezed along a tube until it shoots out through the spider's fangs. Different venoms work in different ways – some affect muscles and nerves, leading to cramp and paralysis, while others kill tissue around the bite, resulting in scars that are slow to heal. Only about 100 species of spider have venom that is harmful to people.

Super sight
A jumping spider can spy prey from 30cm away, thanks to four pairs of eyes. The two largest eyes move independently, which is why they appear here in different colours.

Lifeless male, paralyzed by a bite, is parcelled up in silk.

ARACHNID – *an animal such as a spider or scorpion*

> The goliath bird-eating spider of South America is the world's largest spider, with a legspan of 26cm.

A female black widow prepares to eat her mate.

☢ SECRET WEAPON

Bird-eating spiders, or tarantulas, can give a painful bite. To attack, they raise the front of the body with legs high in the air, and then strike down using their fangs like pickaxes. Some tarantulas release clouds of hairs from their legs. These have microscopic barbs that stick in the skin – or eye – and are very hard to remove.

http://australianmuseum.net.au/spiders

Underside of female's rounded abdomen has red, hourglass-shaped marking.

On the boat from Brazil
Known for its speed and aggression, the Brazilian wandering spider is one of the world's deadliest spiders. It sometimes turns up in Europe hidden among bananas shipped from Central and South America.

pedipalp – sensory feeler for tasting food

Dangerous Australian
The Sydney funnel web spider wanders into houses in towns and cities. It bites with fangs strong enough to pierce a fingernail. Victims must find a doctor fast – the venom can kill in under two hours.

HABITAT – the surroundings that a particular species needs to survive

AMBUSH!

Predatory invertebrates lie in wait for prey, often using camouflage to great effect. Some brightly coloured crab spiders look exactly like a flower, and inject a powerful poison to kill insects larger than themselves. Assassin bugs stab flies, mosquitoes and caterpillars, paralysing them. And ichneumon wasps parasitize their prey, laying their eggs in the larvae and pupae of other insects. The larvae eat their hosts from the inside.

STABBED TO DEATH

Robber flies sit very still somewhere where they can see all around them with their large eyes. When potential food flies past, these large flies (up to 5cm in length) spring off their perch and capture their prey in flight. They have a strong, piercing proboscis and spiny legs that help them hold onto struggling prey.

A robber fly sucks at its blue beetle prey.

An orchid mantis on an orchid flower in Malaysia.

mantis lies in wait looking exactly like a petal

unsuspecting fly is seized when it lands

Predatory mantis

One of the most extraordinary animal camouflages is that of the praying mantis – so-called because it holds its front legs up as if it is 'praying'. These insects live in tropical areas and individual species are often camouflaged to match plants in their habitat.

> There are about 37,500 different known species of spiders in the world.

The trapdoor is made of soil and vegetation, and hinged with silk.

http://insected.arizona.edu/mantidinfo.htm

"'Will you walk into my parlour?'
Said a spider to a fly;
'Tis the prettiest little parlour
That ever you did spy.'"

Mary Howitt (1799–1888)
British poet, from her poem 'The Spider and the Fly' *(1829)*

A trapdoor spider pushes the 'door' aside to seize its prey.

The spider has to be quick to catch a cricket.

Hiding in wait

The trapdoor spider is well named. Instead of spinning a web, it constructs a trapdoor at the entrance to a moist underground burrow. It digs out spaces for hiding and raising young, and lines the burrow with silk. When prey passes overhead, the spider feels the vibrations and throws open the trapdoor to catch its food.

door is chiselled by fangs to match tunnel entrance exactly

spider uses fangs to dig out long burrows

KILLER COLONY

COLONY – *a large group of animals that live together*

Which animals form an army and eat every creature in their path? Army ants, which live in the Americas. They march on a million feet across the jungle floor. Cockroaches, scorpions, tarantulas, crickets – all run for their lives. When an army ant finds its prey, it releases a chemical that 'calls out' to its comrades. In seconds, hundreds of ants arrive to sting the victim, dismember its body and carry it back to the nest.

● ANT IN CLOSE-UP

An ant's body has three parts – a head, thorax and abdomen. The head has the mouth, eyes and antennae. The mouth has two scissor-like jaws called mandibles. Army ants are blind and rely on their antennae to smell, touch and communicate.

thorax

head

abdomen

"Go to the ant, you lazybones; consider its ways, and be wise."

Proverbs 6.6, in the Old Testament of the Bible

Ant food

Army ants feed mainly on other insects, but will kill lizards and snakes. Driver ants, which also form colonies but live in Africa, can smother and kill animals as large as chickens, pigs and goats if they are cooped up or tethered.

> A single colony of army ants can kill and eat up to 100,000 insects in a day.

www.dandelion.org/de/ant

Antbirds perch above the ants, ready to pick off insects fleeing the colony.

Living nests

As army ants move around the forest, they use their own bodies to build temporary night-time nests called bivouacs. The queen and her eggs are safe in the middle of the mass of ants.

In a tangle

Ants use their own bodies to build bridges – for example, linking a bivouac to the ground. The individual ants cling together with their clawed feet.

Large robber fly is ready to snatch any injured insects.

Each ant finds its way by detecting chemicals given off by other ants.

Army on the march

A column of army ants snakes across the leaf litter. At the front of the column, the soldiers fan out, covering an area 10m wide. Prey creatures are stung, then hacked to pieces by the ants' jaws. The army makes thousands of kills a day.

INVESTIGATE

Find out more about creepy crawlies and the environments in which they live by visiting zoos and wildlife parks or by watching and reading about these amazing killer creatures in documentaries, films and reference books.

Wildlife parks and zoos

Visit your nearest zoo where you can get close to many insects and spiders. If you have a fear of spiders, many places offer the chance to handle less dangerous insects to help you overcome any fears.

 Ultimate Bugopedia by Darlyne Murawski and Nancy Honovich (National Geographic Kids)

 ZSL London Zoo, Regent's Park, London, NW1 4RY, UK

www.scorpionworlds.com

jumping spider

African praying mantis eating a bug

Books and magazines

If you want to know more about killer creepy crawlies, check out some of the many reference books and magazines at your local library. Your local librarian may also be able to suggest some great books.

 *The Big Bug Search* by Ian Jackson and Caroline Young (Usborne)

 Ask questions online on the Natural History Museum Bug forum. www.nhm.ac.uk/natureplus/community/identification/bug-forum

 http://insects.about.com/od/roachesandmantids/a/10-Fascinating-Facts-About-Praying-Mantids.htm

Museums and exhibitions

Natural history museums have displays and expert information about all sorts of insects and spiders as well as curators to give tours and bring the exhibits to life.

 Arachnids by Janet Beccaloni (Natural History Museum)

 Bugs Alive! at the Melbourne Museum, 11 Nicholson Street, Carlton, Victoria 3053, Australia

 www.uksafari.com/spiders.htm

red ant army swarming a ladybird

tiny praying mantis

Documentaries and movies

If you can't actually travel to Africa or Australia, do the next best thing and watch documentaries on these places or view photographs by wildlife photographers.

 Madagascar (BBC Films)

 The BBC Nature website has loads of interesting information about creepy crawlies available for free – www.bbc.co.uk/nature/life/Arachnid

 http://animals.nationalgeographic.com/animals/bugs

PREHISTORIC
KILLERS

DINOSAUR – a member of an extinct family of land reptiles that lived from 230 to 65 million years ago

EXTINCT KILLERS

About 100 million years ago, in the swamps of what is now Argentina, there lived a terrifying predator – *Giganotosaurus*. With its huge head, 20 centimetre-long teeth, clawed hands and massive, muscular legs, *Giganotosaurus* probably takes the title as the scariest of all the meat-eating dinosaurs. It was even bigger than its North American cousin, *Tyrannosaurus rex*.

Sail-like structure on back may have been used to regulate body temperature, or for display.

Ferocious theropod

All carnivorous dinosaurs belong to a group that scientists call theropods. *Spinosaurus* was a huge theropod – perhaps as long as 18m – that lived in north Africa 95 million years ago. With its long, crocodilian head, it probably fished rather than hunting on land.

"A single *Giganotosaurus* – even a huge alpha male – is no match for a mature *Argentinosaurus*."

Henry Gee (born 1962)
British palaeontologist

whip-like tail

Following the herd

Giganotosaurus probably lived in small family groups, stalking herds of *Argentinosaurus* and other giant plant-eaters as they moved to new feeding grounds. At 35m long, an adult *Argentinosaurus* was too large to bring down, but small teams of *Giganotosaurus* worked together to pick off younger members of the herd.

 Giganotosaurus, whose name means 'giant southern lizard', probably measured 14m from nose to tail.

Deinonychus foot with outsize claw

Anatomy of a killer

With its long hind legs and light bone structure, *Deinonychus* was a fast sprinter. Each of its feet had one huge, curved claw for hooking into prey.

Argentinosaurus *was a sauropod, a long-necked, plant-eating dinosaur.*

1.8m-long skull, attached to jawbone lined with 20cm-long serrated teeth

● PACK HUNTERS

Deinonychus was an intelligent, speedy, wolf-sized predator. It hunted in packs, stalking and ambushing prey. Members of the pack leapt at their victim in a co-ordinated attack, hanging on with hook-like claws as they bit into the flesh. In this way, *Deinonychus* could hunt prey big enough to provide food for several days.

downy feathers for warmth

powerful legs for sprinting

http://www.nhm.ac.uk/jdsml/nature-online/dino-directory/

Heavy tail helps to counterbalance the enormous head.

huge rear leg muscles braced
Tyrannosaurus rex while it fed

skin may have
had scattered
feathers

Tower of strength

With teeth measuring up to 30cm long, *Tyrannosaurus rex* had a 'bite-and-tear' feeding technique that made short work of fallen flesh. Unlike many predatory dinosaurs, its upper jaw ended in a blunt, U-shaped snout. This enabled it to tear off up to 75kg of food at one go – about the same weight as an average man. It towered over its food on its colossal back legs, while its tiny front legs hung in the air. For a dinosaur, its sense of smell was unusually good, helping it to track down dead food.

large openings between
skull bones helped to reduce
weight of head

> **SCAVENGER** – *an animal that feeds mainly or entirely on dead remains*

DEATH ON TWO LEGS

Tyrannosaurus rex is the world's most famous predator, even though it vanished over 65 million years ago. We know exactly what it looked like thanks to some incredible fossil finds. One of them, nicknamed 'Sue', is amazingly well preserved – a sign that it was covered by mud or sand just after it died. But *Tyrannosaurus rex's* lifestyle remains a puzzle. Instead of being a serial killer, it may have got some or all of its food by scavenging from dead remains.

teeth at front of jaw had a backward curve and a D-shaped cross section

KILLERS COMPARED

Tyrannosaurus rex weighed up to 7 tonnes, and measured up to 13m from head to tail. Despite this, it was probably not the largest land predator of all time. *Carcharodontosaurus* may have weighed over 10 tonnes, while *Giganotosaurus* tipped the scales at over 12 tonnes. The longest of all may have been *Spinosaurus* – a sail-backed hunter with jaws like a crocodile, which is thought to have fed on fish. It may have been up to 18m long.

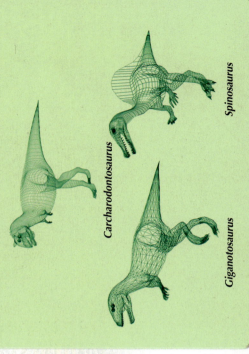

Spinosaurus

Carcharodontosaurus

Giganotosaurus

> In 2009, palaeontologists identified a miniature tyrannosaur, called *Raptorex*. It weighed only a hundredth as much as *Tyrannosaurus rex.*

COLOUR AND DISGUISE

A huge amount is known about dinosaur skeletons, but no one knows what dinosaur bodies would have looked like from the outside. Traditionally, they are often painted a plain grey, like gigantic rhinos or elephants. However, small dinosaurs – such as *Coelophysis* – may well have been brightly coloured, like many lizards are today. Bold patterns would have broken up their outline, helping them to blend in with their background as they stalked their prey.

Coelophysis **may have had brightly coloured, patterned skin that camouflaged them amongst the shadows of the undergrowth.**

🔴 SOFT TOUCH

Living reptiles are all covered with scales. Although dinosaurs were reptiles, fossils of some species – such as *Sinosauropteryx* – show that they were covered with fine, fuzzy down. Others had simple feathers, even though they could not fly. These body coverings might have been brightly coloured, helping dinosaurs to attract partners when the time came to mate.

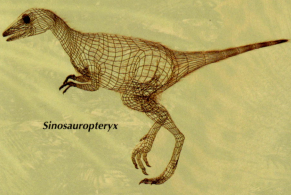

Sinosauropteryx

> Dinosaur colours were produced by chemical pigments, such as melanin, stored inside cells in their skin.

Out of the shadows

This group of *Coelophysis* is feeding on a kill. Their markings look eye-catching in the open, but they would have worked as camouflage in sun-dappled shade. *Coelophysis* may have had different markings in males and females, and another set of markings that helped adults to identify their young. These juvenile markings would have changed when the young became ready to breed. Some dinosaurs may also have changed colour to express their mood – a trick used by chameleons and other modern lizards.

http://news.bbc.co.uk/1/hi/7124969.stm

Mummified skin

When dinosaurs died, their soft body parts usually rotted before they became fossilized. But sometimes, a dinosaur's body would dry out, forming a mummified corpse. One of these 'dinomummies' shows the knobbly pattern of a hadrosaur's skin in an amazing amount of detail for something over 65 million years old.

WARM-BLOODED – *having a body that stays at a steady warm temperature, whatever the conditions outside*

PACK ATTACK

Plant-eating dinosaurs weren't the only ones that often lived in groups. Some fast, quick-witted killers worked like wolves in a pack, singling out prey many times their own size. One of these was *Deinonychus* – a predator that used extra-large hind claws to attack its victims. Measuring about three metres long, *Deinonychus* was light enough to leap aboard its prey. Here, it set to work with its claws, bringing much bigger dinosaurs crashing to the ground.

Winning formula

Small pack-hunting killers lived throughout the Dinosaur Age. One of the earliest was *Coelophysis*. At Ghost Ranch, in New Mexico, thousands of *Coelophysis* fossils have been found together. The fossils come in two sizes – scientists think that the larger ones are males.

Deinonychus

hands had three fingers, tipped with long claws

One against many

In a forest clearing, about 100 million years ago, a plant-eating *Tenontosaurus* is fighting for its life as a pack of *Deinonychus* slash at it with their claws. Unlike early dinosaurs, *Deinonychus* was probably warm-blooded. A covering of feathers would have kept in its body heat, enabling it to stay active even in cold conditions. Warm-blooded animals make effective hunters, but they need more fuel than cold-blooded ones to keep their bodies working. As a result, the *Deinonychus* pack would be constantly on the hunt.

> *Deinonychus*'s sickle-shaped rear claws were about 12cm long.

second toe swivelled
downwards when
Deinonychus *attacked*

Tenontosaurus

extra-large claw on second
toe stayed off the ground
when Deinonychus *was on
the move, keeping it sharp*

OSTEODERM – *a large, raised scale that is reinforced by a layer of bone*

FIGHTING BACK

For plant-eating dinosaurs, survival meant being permanently on guard. If they were attacked, very few could use their teeth as weapons. Instead, some hit back by rearing up on their back legs, or by stabbing their opponents with sharp claws. *Ankylosaurus* had some of the best protection of all. The dinosaur was covered in armour plating, and its stiff tail ended in a massive club that could smash an enemy's skull.

Deadly spikes

Stegosaurus had bony plates on its back, but its real weapons were vicious spikes on its sides and at the tip of its tail. The spikes pointed outwards, so they stabbed into an enemy as *Stegosaurus* swung around.

tail spikes

Killer blow

With its 5-tonne body and superb defences, *Ankylosaurus* was built to stand and fight rather than to run away. Here, the dinosaur is fending off an *Albertosaurus* that has unwisely closed in to attack. *Ankylosaurus*'s skin was reinforced and protected with bony plates, or osteoderms, and its tail club could swing with shattering force if anything came too close. Its only weak point was its underside, which had unarmoured skin.

bony plates protected each eye

Ankylosaurus

REARING UP

Sauropods had legs like pillars, and spent almost all of their time on all fours. However, faced with danger, some could rear up on their back legs in a bid to trample an attacker. Many kinds, including *Barosaurus*, had a large claw on the inside of each front foot, which could have ripped downwards into an attacker. However, rearing up could put the huge animal off-balance, sending it crashing to the ground.

***Barosaurus* rearing up**

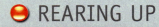

skin is protected by bony plates and knobs, or osteoderms

tail club had two large lobes and weighed over 50kg

Albertosaurus

rows of extra-large plates ran along back and sides

Scissorhands

Therizinosaurus had the longest claws ever known – they could be nearly 1m long. They might have worked as weapons, but their main job was probably gathering plant food.

INVESTIGATE

Find out more about dangerous dinosaurs by visiting museums and fossil-hunting sites or by watching and reading about these awe-inspiring reptiles in documentaries, movies and reference books.

boy viewing dinosaur skeletons

Museums and exhibitions

Most of the world's greatest dinosaur fossils are displayed in museums, giving you a chance to come face to face with these giants from the past.

 Dinosaur Hunters (Natural History Museum)

 Natural History Museum, Cromwell Road, London SW7 5BD, UK

 http://australianmuseum.net.au/event/dinosaurs

Tyrannosaurus rex

Fossil-hunting sites

Try hunting for fossils in your local area at rocky places inland or at the seaside. Head for areas that have sedimentary (layered) rocks. If you are at the coast, keep safe by staying away from cliffs and always get the latest information about local tides.

 KFK Rocks and Fossils by Margaret Hynes (Kingfisher)

 The Jurassic Coast, which runs along England's south coast from Devon to Dorset, is famous for fossils. Charmouth Beach, part of the Golden Cap estate, is a great starting place.

 www.nationaltrust.org.uk/article-1355830164461

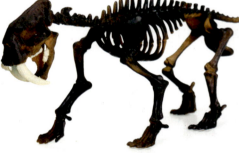

sabre-toothed tiger skeleton

Books and magazines

If you are fascinated by dinosaurs and other prehistoric animals, it's hard to beat illustrated reference books. Many magazines contain up-up-to-the-minute news about dinosaur discoveries.

 The Kingfisher Dinosaur Encyclopedia
Michael Benton (Kingfisher)

 Subscribe to dinosaur information magazines such as *Dinosaur Action* – www.dinomitemag.com

model of a *Tyrannosaurus rex* at Sirindhorn museum, Thailand

www.nhm.ac.uk/nature-online/life/dinosaurs-other-extinct-creatures

Documentaries and movies

You can't visit the Dinosaur Age, but thanks to computerized animation, documentaries and movies, the distant past can seem amazingly real.

 Walking with Dinosaurs (BBC Films)

 Earth's Dinosaur Zoo, a live entertainment and educational dinosaur show http://dinosaurzoolive.com

 www.bbc.co.uk/sn/prehistoric_life/dinosaurs/seamonsters

GLOSSARY

abdomen
In animals such as insects and arachnids, the tail end of the body.

algae (singular: alga)
Simple non-flowering plants that grow in water or moist surroundings.

amphibian
A cold-blooded animal that lives on land but breeds in water, for example a frog.

antenna (plural: antennae)
In insects, one of a pair of sensory feelers that stick out from the head.

antivenin
A substance containing antibodies that counteract the effects of animal venom.

bacterium (plural: bacteria)
A simple micro-organism. Some bacteria can cause disease.

binocular vision
Seeing that involves two eyes working together, allowing the viewer to judge distances. The eyes face forwards to give overlapping fields of view.

bioluminescence
The production of light by living things, to be found in fish and insects as well as simple animals that live in the sea.

blubber
The thick layer of fat beneath a sea mammal's skin that keeps its body warm in the extreme cold.

camouflage
Shapes and colours that help an animal to blend in with its background, so that it can hide from its enemies or get close to its prey.

canine teeth
Also known as fangs or dogteeth, the four pointed teeth at the front of a mammal's mouth on either side of its incisors, used for gripping meat.

canopy
The highest part of a rainforest, where the trees spread out their branches.

carcass
The dead body of an animal.

carnassial teeth
The large teeth near the back of a carnivore's jaw, used for shearing at flesh and bone.

carnivorous
Describes a flesh-eating animal, especially one from the Carnivora order, which includes dogs, cats and bears.

carrion
The flesh of a dead animal.

cold-blooded
Describes an animal that cannot control its own body temperature, which changes according to the surroundings.

disembowelled
Describes a body when its vital organs have been ripped out.

down
A layer of short, fluffy feathers that feathered dinosaurs used to keep warm and birds still have today.

echolocation
The way that some animals, such as bats, find their way and locate prey, by making sounds and using the returned echoes to work out their surroundings.

extinct
Describes an animal or plant that has died out globally, never to reappear.

fossil
Remains of living things that have been preserved in the ground. In most fossils, the original remains are replaced by hard minerals, which can keep their shape for millions of years.

gland
A group of cells or an organ in the body that produces a particular substance, such as poison.

incisors
A mammal's sharp-edged front teeth, used for scraping meat from bones or cutting vegetable matter.

invertebrate
An animal that does not have a backbone.

larva (plural: larvae)
The second stage in the life of an insect, between the egg and the adult.

ligament
Tough, fibrous tissue that connects muscle to bone.

mammal
An animal that gives birth to live young, which feed on mother's milk. Lions and bears are mammals.

mandibles
In insects, mouthparts used for biting and crushing food.

marrow
Fatty, protein-rich tissue that fills the hollow centre of bones.

mimic
An animal that copies another, often in order to avoid being eaten.

molars
The broad teeth found at the back of a mammal's jaw, used for grinding food.

nematocyst
A tiny stinging cell that injects venom into prey or an attacker. Jellyfish are armed with nematocysts.

nocturnal
Describes an animal that is active mainly at night and sleeps during the day.

palaeontologist
A scientist who studies the fossils (preserved remains) of extinct animals.

paralysis
A state in which the body, or part of the body, loses the ability to move or feel. Venom can cause paralysis and, in some cases, death.

parasitize
To live on another animal, taking nutrients from that animal's body.

pigments
Coloured chemicals that are found in rocks as well as in living things.

polyp
A tiny aquatic creature with a tube-shaped body. Coral reefs build up gradually from the leftover skeletons of dead polyps.

predator
An animal that hunts and kills other animals.

prehistoric
Something that existed before recorded history began.

prey
Animals that are hunted by others as food. Plant-eating dinosaurs were prey animals, but so were many predatory dinosaurs, because they were hunted by dinosaurs larger than themselves.

proboscis
A long, flexible snout.

pupa (plural: pupae)
The resting, non-feeding stage during the life cycle of an insect when it transforms from a larva into an adult.

rainforest
A thick forest, with very tall trees, that grows in tropical countries where it is hot all year round and rains every day.

reptile
A cold-blooded animal with scaly skin, for example a snake. Some reptiles lay eggs and others give birth to live young.

saliva
Liquid produced in the mouth to make food easier to swallow.

savannah
An area of grassland and scattered trees, found in tropical or subtropical regions.

scavenger
An animal that feeds on carrion.

stoop
To swoop down, for example a hawk diving down to catch a rabbit.

subtropical
Found in the subtropics – the warm region between the hot tropics closer to the equator, and the cooler, temperate parts of the world.

talons
The sharp claws of birds of prey that they use to snatch up their quarry.

theropod
A two-legged, carnivorous dinosaur with extremely sharp teeth and claws. All theropods belonged to the saurischian, or lizard-hipped, group of dinosaurs.

thorax
In animals such as insects, the middle part of the body, found between the head and abdomen.

toxin
A poisonous substance, especially one formed in the body.

tropical
Found in the tropics – the hot parts of the world on either side of the Equator.

venom
The poisonous fluid that some animals, such as snakes, inject into their prey.

vertebrae (singular: vertebra)
Bones that link together to form the backbone, or spine, of an animal.

vertebrate
An animal that has a backbone.

INDEX